What Grandma Said

Published by Kudu Publishing

Cover design by: Bernardo Abraham

ISBN: 978-1-954089-67-9 1 2 3 4 5 6 7 8 9 10

Printed in the United States of America

What Grandma Said

100 SAYINGS OF WISDOM

KAY A. RIDDLE

DEDICATION

To my mother, Shirley Ann Gregory, whom I love and miss so much. You always inspired me to do my best and told me I could do anything.

To my grandmother, Momma, I pray I will never forget your wise sayings.

ACKNOWLEDGMENTS

I would like to thank my Lord and Savior, Jesus Christ, my Rock and Foundation.

I would also like to thank my husband, Daniel, who loves me, sees the gifts that God has given me, tells me how smart I am, and believes I can do whatever I put my mind to. Thank you for supporting me, never pressuring me about getting a job, and allowing me the time to write this book. Love you!

This book is in remembrance of Grandmother—better known to me as "Momma." To others, she is known as Grandma, Grandma Katy, Cousin Katy, Miss Katy, Aunt Katy, or just Katy. My grandmother had a word of wisdom for any situation in life. I really thought she had eyes "in the back of her head," as she would say when she would ask me what I was doing behind her back. We often sit around and say, “What did Grandma say?” about a situation. Thank you so much, Momma, for all that wisdom.

My aunt Elsie Mae has been an inspiration and motivation to me. She always encouraged me and saw me the way that God sees me. Thank you, Auntie, for all your input.

To my sister Carla: words can’t express what you have been to me as I was writing this book. You were always praying and encouraging me. Sis, you never once in the last five years stopped believing in me. Thank you for all your input as well.

To my daughter, Kaysha: you’re my biggest cheerleader and think your mom is the greatest. Thank you for editing and all that you did to help me get this book out.

CONTENTS

INTRODUCTION

My prayer is that this book would be a legacy for my family to pass on to their children and grandchildren who will never meet Momma, Grandma, Big Mama, Nana, or whatever you called her. I also pray that when others read this book, it would bring back memories of their grandmothers as well. God bless every buyer and reader in Jesus' Name.

WISDOM

Wisdom is the principal thing; therefore, get wisdom. And in all getting, get understanding.
–Proverbs 4:7 (NKJV)

I do not remember my grandmother reading the Bible, but there was one in the house. We were made to go to church because we "needed religion." I guess that's what being saved was called back then. Even though she didn't attend church, she was very wise. I would laugh or shake my head because I thought she was making up some of these sayings as she went along. Some did not make any sense to me at the time. Now, as I read the Bible, I see that a lot of what she was saying wasn't just old wives' tales. Some of it was actually Scripture (paraphrased).

A FEW SAYINGS ABOUT WISDOM:

A lady should be seen and not heard. (Self-control)

~

Don't curse the bridge that brought you over. (Be careful how you treat people.)

~

Don't talk too much. (It's best they think you are a fool than you open your mouth, and now they know it.)

~

You going to let your mouth write a check that your behind can't cash. (Boasting)

~

Lying straight through your teeth. (Not telling the truth.)

~

Don't ask me no questions; I tell you no lie. (Don't ask if you don't want the truth.)

~

Tell that to somebody who don't know any better. (Don't make up a story to try to impress me. I know you.)

~

You need to listen more than you speak.
(You talk too much.)

~

Don't tell all your business;
keep some things to yourselves.
(Be quiet sometime.)

~

A still tongue make a wise head.
(Don't talk too much.)

~

You can't hold water. (Telling secrets.)

~

Keep your word.
(Be a person of integrity.)

~

If you say you are going to do it, then do it. (Don't commit to something you know you are not going to do.)

~

Close your mouth before a fly fly into it.
(Acting surprised.)

~

A child should be seen and not heard.
(Children should be quiet.)

~

Keep lying; the Lord will strike you dead. (A saying Grandma used.)

~

Tell the truth; shame the devil. (A saying Grandma used.)

~

If I told you once, I have told you twice. (Warning)

~

Keep talking; you're digging a bigger hole for yourself. (The more a person talks, the more trouble they get themselves in.)

~

A still tongue make a wise head.
(It's wise not to talk a lot.)

~

Got a mouth like a motor.
(Talk all the time.)

~

Keep rolling your eyes, they going to fall out. (A saying Grandma used.)

~

PRAYER:

Father God, we know some of these are old wives' tales, but there is truth to so much. Lord, help us to discern what is good for us and what is not. You said wisdom was the principal thing, so get wisdom, and with my getting, get understanding. You said if I lack wisdom, I can ask You, Lord, and You will give it to me as long as I do not doubt. I ask You, Lord, for wisdom, and I receive the wisdom of God for my life in Jesus' Name. Thank You, Lord, for wisdom.

The beginning of wisdom is this: Get wisdom,
and whatever you get, get insight.
– Proverbs 4:27 (ESV)

If any of you lacks wisdom, let him ask of
God, who gives to all liberally and without
reproach, and it will be given to him.
–James 1:5 (NKJV)

KINDNESS

And be ye kind one to another, tenderhearted, forgiving one another, even as God for Christ's sake hath forgiven you.
–Ephesians 4:32 (KJV)

My grandmother believed in treating people right no matter how they treated her. She'd tell us, "Being kind to someone will take you a long way." She would say to us, "Treat people the way you want to be treated." If someone was not kind to us, she sometimes would tell us, "That might be the way that person was raised."

A FEW SAYINGS ABOUT KINDNESS:

God don't like ugly.
(She was talking about attitude.)

Give me my roses while I'm living.
(Treat me right while I'm living.)

You can catch more bees with
honey than you can with dung.
(Kindness can win a person.)

Kill them with kindness. (Being kind possibly will soften a cold person.)

~

Mind your business, and leave other people's alone. (Stay out of people's business.)

~

Being kind will take you a long way. (Showing kindness will take you further than being mean.)

~

You can catch more flies with honey than with vinegar. (A saying Grandma used.)

~

Don't throw stones.
(Don't talk about someone else.)

~

Think before you speak.
(Don't react. Think, then reply.)

~

Look the other way. (Forgiveness)

~

PRAYER:

Father God, thank You for Your loving kindness that drew me to You. Now, Father, teach me to be kind and compassionate to everyone I come in contact with. Help me to quickly forgive the way You have forgiven me. Teach me to love my enemies and do good to all I meet, expecting nothing in return because my reward is with You and comes from You.

The Lord has appeared of old to me, saying: "Yes, I have loved you with an everlasting love; Therefore with lovingkindness I have drawn you."
–Jeremiah 31:3 (NKJV)

Love your enemies, and do good, and lend, expecting nothing in return, and your reward will be great, and you will be sons of the Most High, for he is kind to the ungrateful and the evil.
–Ephesians 4:32 (NIV)

CAUTION

Look carefully then how you walk, not as unwise but as wise, making the best use of the time, because the days are evil. Therefore do not be foolish, but understand what the will of the Lord is.
–Ephesians 5:15-17 (ESV)

When my grandmother advised us on being cautious, she might say, "Be careful: who you hang out with, where you are going, whose house you visit." "Don't tell everything you know."

Sometimes she would tell us that our friends were not really our friends, or they didn't mean us any good. Or she would say, "Be careful of that one," talking about a particular person.

A FEW SAYINGS ABOUT CAUTION:

Feed them with a long-handle spoon.
(Someone who has betrayed you.)

Don't let the left hand know
what the right hand is doing.
(Do some things in secret.)

Keep your ears open because the night
do not have eyes. (Stay alert.)

Use your head for more than a hat rack. (Use your brain.)

~

Believe half of what you see and none of what you hear. (Do not be so quick to believe everything.)

~

A dog that brings a bone will carry a bone. (Gossipers will talk about you also.)

~

If I told you to go jump off a bridge, would you do it? (Think for yourself.)

~

Don't overstep your boundaries.
(Be respectful.)

~

The jury is still out on that one.
(I don't know if I believe it.)

~

What you do in the dark will come to light. (You cannot hide the truth.)

~

These walls have ears.
(Someone is always listening.)

~

Don't stir up mess because it will stink. (Do not keep bringing up old stuff.)

~

An idle mind is the devil's workshop. (A saying of my grandmother.)

~

Quit grinning so much like a chess[hire] cat. (A saying of my grandmother from Alice in Wonderland.)

~

Grass is not always greener on the other side. (Do not envy someone else. Life might not be as smooth as it looks.)

~

Don't put all your eggs in one basket. (Always have a back-up plan.)

~

Big pictures got little ears. (Photographs do talk.)

~

I'd like to be a fly on the wall. (To hear someone else's private conversation.)

~

Don't cut your nose off to spite your face. (Don't act too quickly.)

~

A hard head make a soft bottom. (Disciplining)

Close the door; you don't live in a barn. (A saying grandma used.)

What don't come out in the wash will come out in the rinse. (The more they tell their story, eventually the truth will come out.)

PRAYER:

Father God, help me to heed Your ways. Help me to be careful how I walk, not as an unwise person—but as someone who is wise. Help me to take notice of my actions and not to be high-minded—but to walk humbly before You. Lord, I don't want to be a person that leads someone astray—but guides righteously. Thank You for the Holy Spirit that will lead and guide me as I guide others to the truth in Jesus' Name. Thank You, Jesus.

Therefore be careful how you walk, not as unwise men but as wise.
—Ephesians 5:15 (NASB)

Therefore let him who thinks he stands take heed that he does not fall.
—1 Corinthians 10:12 (NASB)

The righteous is a guide to his neighbor,
But the way of the wicked leads them astray.
—Proverbs 12:26 (NASB)

HUMILITY

Humble yourselves therefore under the mighty hand of God, that he may exalt you in due time.
–1 Peter 5:6 (KJV)

Momma would say things like, "Keep walking with your head up in the air, you going to trip over something." "The higher you go up, the harder you fall." "Keep acting like that; God has a way of bringing you down." She told us she used to say, "I remember when you used a pee pot for a hat!" Now, that was funny.

A FEW SAYINGS ABOUT CAUTION:

A sight for sore eyes. (Happy to see one you have not seen in a while.)

You children are dumb as a doorknob. (Not thinking.)

You keep on living, for [you] haven't heard it all. (Do not think you know it all.)

Come hell or high water.
(Keep your word, no matter what.)

~

Crazy as a bed bug.
(Not making sense.)

~

Dog kiss my foot. (I told you so.)

~

Teeth and tongues fall out, so
know people going to fall out.
(Friends will let you down.)

~

You don't have a wing or a prayer or a leg to stand on. (You're in trouble.)

~

You think you are all that!
I remember when you used
a pee pot for a hat. (Pride)

~

You just as crooked as
two left shoes. (Lying)

~

The tales always turn.
(The truth will come out.)

~

You can't tell the night from day. (Ignorant)

~

Give them enough rope, they hang themselves. (Let people keep talking, and they will entrap themselves.)

~

People in Africa wished they had this food. (She didn't want us to be wasteful.)

~

I'd like to open that head and see what's inside. (Foolish talk.)

~

Where is your head? (Not thinking.)

~

Keep on living; you haven't seen it all.
(Keep watching for new things.)

~

Eating high off the hog. (Pride)

~

You can't get blood from a turnip.
(When you don't have money.)

~

Pot calling the kettle black. (Hypocrisy)

~

Big pictures got little ears.
(You never know who is listening.)

~

Don't toot your own horn. (Pride)

~

Eyes bigger than your stomach. (Greed)

~

Smell like a muskrat. (Sweaty person.)

~

Running around like a chicken with the head cut off. (A saying grandma used.)

~

I brought you in this world, and I'll take you out. (A saying grandma used.)

~

A piece of job is better than no job at all. (Wisdom)

~

Walking on thin ice. (Warning)

~

You don't have a leg to stand on. (Lying)

~

Don't have a pot to pee in and window to throw it out. (Pride)

~

You think you got eyes in the back of your head. (See too much.)

~

So broke [you] don't have two nickels to rub together. (A saying grandma used.)

~

PRAYER:

Father God, forgive me for pride, and show me any area of my life where I have thought myself better than someone else. I humble myself that You might exalt me. Thank You, Lord, for being near to the brokenhearted and saving those that are crushed in spirit. Lord, You resist the proud and give grace to the humble. I can do nothing without You, but I can do all things through Christ who strengthen me in Jesus' Name.

Whoever exalts himself will be humbled, and
whoever humbles himself will be exalted.
–Matthew 23:12 (ESV)

The LORD is near to the brokenhearted
and saves the crushed in spirit.
–Psalm 34:18 (ESV)

Humble yourselves in the sight of the
Lord, and He will lift you up.
–James 4:10 (NKJV)

But He gives more grace. Therefore He says: "God
resists the proud, But gives grace to the humble."
–James 4:6 (NKJV)

POSITIVITY

Greater is he that is in you, than he that is in the world.
—1 John 4:4 (KJV)

My grandma would say that if you were not cheerful in the morning, you should say, "Thank God for waking me up." If we didn't eat all our food, she would say, "The children in ______ ____________________________________ are hungry." (She would call the country's name out, but because I don't want to offend anyone, I will not mention the name.)

A FEW SAYINGS ABOUT POSITIVITY:

It's more than one way to skin a cat. (There is more than one way to get something done.)

Good things come to those who wait. (Have patience.)

Be patient. God didn't create the world in one day. (Have patience.)

I got a bigger fish to fry.
(Not important right now.)

~

A woman's hair is her glory. (Truth)

~

What goes on in this house stays in this house. (A saying grandma used.)

~

Don't beat a dead horse. (Let it go!)

~

You can lead a horse to water,
but you can't make it drink it.
(All you can do is show it.)

~

You made that bed; now you have to sleep in it. (Bad decisions.)

~

You can't make folks do nothing they don't want to do it. (Laziness)

~

Count your blessings. (Wisdom)

~

A bird in the hand is worth two in a bush. (Be grateful for what you have.)

~

Two heads are better than one—even if it's a cabbage head. (Getting wisdom.)

~

Half your day gone by noon. (Don't waste time.)

~

Blacker the berry, sweeter the juice. (When blackberries are ripe.)

~

PRAYER:

Thank You, Lord, that I can do all things through Christ Who strengthens me. No matter the task, God will strengthen me for it. Thank You for supplying every one of my needs–salvation, shelter, clothing, food, wealth, health, and peace of mind–according to Your riches in glory. Thank You for the measure of faith and that it is being increased daily by studying and hearing the Word of God. I don't have to fear because greater is He that is within me than he that is in the world.

I can do all things through Christ which strengtheneth me.
–Philippians 4:13 (KJV)

My God shall supply all your need according
to His riches in glory by Christ Jesus.
– Philippians 4:19 (NKJV)

God hath not given us the spirit of fear; but of
power, and of love, and of a sound mind.
–2 Timothy 1:7 (KJV)

God hath dealt to every man the measure of faith.
– Romans 12:3 (KJV)

The people who know their God shall
be strong and do exploits.
– Daniel 11:32 (KJV)

ABOUT THE AUTHOR

Kay A. Gregory Riddle is a wife, a mother, and a Glam-ma to a beautiful granddaughter.

She grew up in the picturesque city of Lackey, Virginia, with her five beautiful sisters and handsome brother. God has allowed her to travel the world with her husband, Daniel.

When asked about the most important things about her, she sincerely proclaims, "I LOVE THE LORD JESUS CHRIST. Without Him, I can do nothing. Thank You, Jesus, for the Holy Spirit—He has helped to me to write this book and more to follow."

www.ingramcontent.com/pod-product-compliance
Lightning Source LLC
LaVergne TN
LVHW020049110826
845155LV00029B/706

* 9 7 8 1 9 5 4 0 8 9 6 7 9 *